Con

Would you be a bee?

You could buzz around
in the sky,

2

a bee's nest

but you would have
to share your home
with many other bees.

3

You could sip nectar from hundreds of flowers,

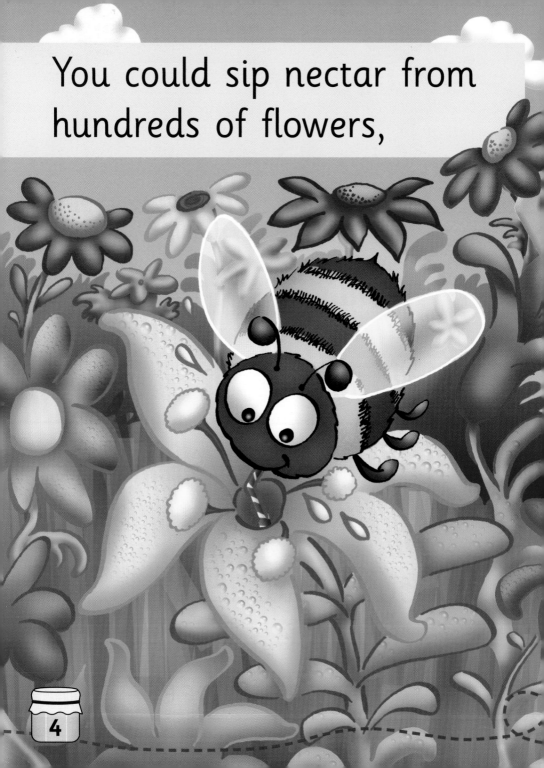

Worker bees carry pollen in the baskets on their back legs.

Pollen

Pollen

but you would have to carry back lots of pollen.

You could show other bees
the way by dancing,

The waggle dance tells the worker
bees where to find flowers.

but you would all have to work hard for the queen bee.

queen bee

You would have five eyes
to help you look for flowers,

compound eyes

8

but you would not be able to see the colour red.

You could find your way
by the sun,

but you would live for only a few weeks.

4 days

Life span
42–49
days

12 days

5 days

Life cycle of a worker bee

You could make golden honey,

honeycomb

but the beekeeper could take it away.

Beekeepers wear special clothes to stop bee stings.

13

15

Index

Would you be a bee?